SPACE DISCOVERY

SUSAN BECKLAKE

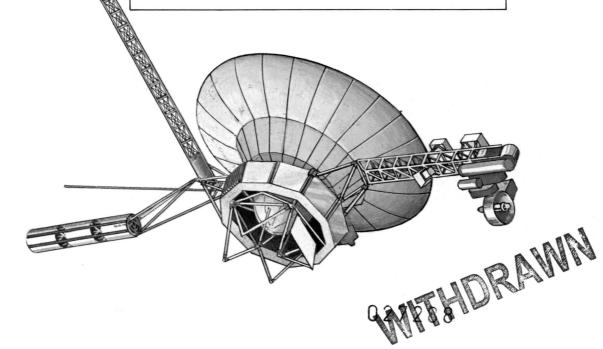

MACDONALD

Editor Susan Simpson
Designer Peter Luff
Illustrated by:
John Bishop
Drawing Attention/Robert Burns
Richard Eastland
Phillip Emms
Richard Hook
Mike Roffe
Barry Salter
Raymond Turvey

Published for Kmart Corporation
Troy, Michigan 48084

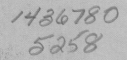

© Theorem Publishing Limited 1980
Conceived and produced by
Theorem Publishing Limited
71-73 Great Portland Street
London W1N 5DH

First published in 1980 by
Macdonald Educational Ltd
Holywell House
Worship Street
London EC2A 2EN

ISBN 0 356 070921

Printed in Hong Kong

Key to cover

1. Skylab was the world's first
space station. It was launched in
1973 and fell back to earth in 1979.
Learn more about Skylab and other
space stations on pages 24, 25, 28
and 29.

2. Astronauts have to wear protective
space suits when they walk in space.
Why? Read more about the problems of
living in space on pages 24 and 25.

3. The Space Shuttle will cut the cost
of space travel. Find out how on
page 22.

4. Titan-Centaur rockets launched the
two Viking space probes sent to Mars

in 1976. The development of rockets
and how they work is described on
pages 22 and 23.

5. A Viking lander probe approaches
Mars. Probes have collected vital
information about many of the planets
in our solar system. For details about
the planets read pages 8 to 13.

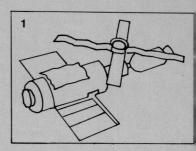

SPACE DISCOVERY

For centuries people have dreamed of voyages to the stars. During the last 20 years or so, we have taken the first steps towards making this dream come true. Probes and satellites feed us information about space every minute of the day; yet there are still objects in space about which we know nothing. This book describes the knowledge we have about the universe and suggests solutions for some of its mysteries. If you are interested in doing some star-gazing yourself turn to the last few pages for some useful tips.

CONTENTS

The Great Unknown	4
Focus on the Sky	6
Our Solar System	8
Worlds of Rock and Ice	10
The Gas Giants	12
First Step – the Moon	14
The Life-giver	16
The Stars	18
Is Anyone Out There?	20
We Have Lift-off!	22
Space Travellers	24
Robot Explorers	26
Space Stations	28
The Sky at Night	30
Index	32

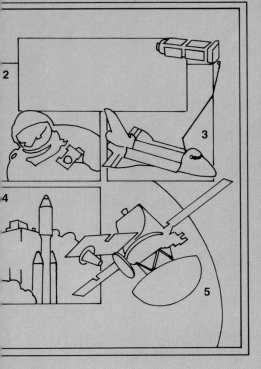

The Great Unknown

It is hard to believe that we live on a large spinning ball that is racing round a star, which is itself speeding through space. The earth seems flat to us and does not appear to be moving. The sun, the moon and the stars look as though they are moving slowly round the earth. Naturally the first men who watched the stars thought the universe really was like this. They were aware of the regular movements of the sun and the moon, and saw the unchanging patterns of the stars. They named groups of stars, or constellations, after mythical beasts and gods. Early astronomers also noticed that a few of the star-like lights moved in strange looping paths across the star patterns. These are the planets. Early men worshipped all these lights in the sky as gods.

Stonehenge is an ancient stone monument in southern England. Built over 3500 years ago, it is a circle of archways made from huge stones. Other arches and stones stand in and near the circle, but many of the stones have fallen or disappeared. We do not know exactly why Stonehenge was built, but it may have been a temple to

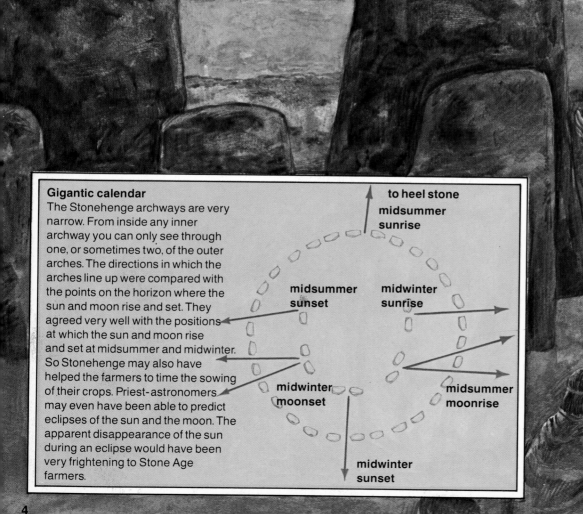

Gigantic calendar
The Stonehenge archways are very narrow. From inside any inner archway you can only see through one, or sometimes two, of the outer arches. The directions in which the arches line up were compared with the points on the horizon where the sun and moon rise and set. They agreed very well with the positions at which the sun and moon rise and set at midsummer and midwinter. So Stonehenge may also have helped the farmers to time the sowing of their crops. Priest-astronomers may even have been able to predict eclipses of the sun and the moon. The apparent disappearance of the sun during an eclipse would have been very frightening to Stone Age farmers.

to heel stone
midsummer sunrise

midsummer sunset

midwinter sunrise

midwinter moonset

midsummer moonrise

midwinter sunset

sun god. If you look through one of
e arches on midsummer day, you
ll see the sun rise over the 'heel
one', a single stone that stands
tside the circle. However, some
tronomers now think Stonehenge
ay have been a very early
servatory for studying the
ovements of the sun and the moon.

Egyptian universe

Ends of the earth

Many early civilizations thought that
the earth was flat. In India they
thought the land was supported by
elephants standing on the back of a
turtle. The Egyptians pictured their
universe filled with gods. The sun
god, Ra, sailed in a boat across the
starry sky goddess, Nut. Over 2000
years ago some Greek thinkers
realized the earth was round, but the
idea was slow to catch on. Even in
1492, when Columbus set off across
the Atlantic Ocean many people
thought he would sail off the edge of
the world.

Centre of the universe

Ancient Greek astronomers tried to
explain the movements of the sun,
moon and planets. Ptolemy
described a universe in which
everything circled around the earth,
but this simple picture could not

explain exactly what he saw. Other
astronomers suggested correctly
that the earth might move around the
sun. But it was Ptolemy's theory that
was accepted. No-one challenged it
for another 1400 years.

Venus

Jupiter

Mars

moon earth

Mercury

sun

Saturn

5

Focus on the Sky

One of the main tools of the modern astronomer is the telescope. An ordinary telescope collects light from distant stars and galaxies. Even with the biggest telescope a star looks like nothing more than a point of light, but that light carries very useful information about the star. It can tell the astronomer what the star is made of and how hot it is, for example. As well as light, stars also give out a whole range of radiation including radio waves and x-rays. Our atmosphere stops most of this radiation from reaching the astronomer on the ground – only light and some radio waves get through. In the last few years astronomers have sent special instruments into space. These can collect more detailed information about the stars and relay it back.

The large optical telescopes on earth use curved mirrors to collect the light. The biggest telescope has a mirror 20 feet across. As the earth spins, the stars appear to move across the sky. The telescope must also move to follow the stars the astronomer wants to study. Telescopes are protected by domes which can open and rotate so that the telescope can point at any part of the sky. Telescopes are usually built at the tops of mountains, above the murky lower atmosphere, and well away from big cities. City lights easily blot out the tiny amounts of light that reach us from far out in space.

Eye on space

When people first began to study the skies they had to rely on their eyes. They first built instruments to plot the positions of the planets. The discovery of the telescope allowed them to study the planets themselves. The next step was the use of photography with the telescope. This was an advance, as the camera can record more accurately than the eye. It can also 'see' fainter stars and further galaxies. The development of the rocket enabled scientists to send telescopes and probes into space.

This observatory in India was built in the 18th century to plot (map out) the movements of the planets.

Galileo was the first scientist to use a telescope. Through it he saw the craters on the moon.

Modern telescopes are giants compared with Galileo's instruments, which he held in his hand.

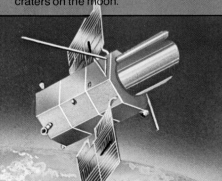

Rockets carry telescopes into space to study the stars from far above our atmosphere.

Men have now explored parts of the moon. They brought back the first rocks from another body in space.

Signals from space

Radio waves from space were first detected in 1932. A radio telescope collects radio waves with its dish rather like the mirror of an optical telescope collects light. The radio waves are reflected to a detector which records the strength and direction of the signal. In 1967 a signal was detected that varied so regularly that astronomers at first thought it was a message from outer space. They had discovered the first pulsar, which may be the remains of a dying star.

dome shutters

mirror

observing chair

control room

Amateur sightings
There are many amateur astronomers. Their small telescopes often cover a large area of the sky, so they can watch for comets approaching the sun. Many comets have been spotted first by amateur astronomers. Also, they are often the first people to notice a nova, a star which suddenly becomes very bright.

Our Solar System

The earth is one of a family of nine planets that circle a star called the sun. This family also includes many asteroids, comets, meteoroids and moons. The sun is by far the largest member, and next in size come the planets. Some of the moons circling the planets are as large as the smallest planets. The smallest moon, Deimos, that revolves round Mars, is only 7½ miles across. Deimos may once have been an asteroid. Asteroids are just chunks of rock that circle the sun mainly in a belt between Mars and Jupiter. In the past few years many new discoveries have been made about the solar system. Several new moons have been discovered, while the giant planets, Jupiter and Uranus, were found to have rings round them like Saturn. Some of these discoveries were made by astronomers here on earth and others by space probes sent to visit the planets.

Cloud of dust

The solar system began as a spinning cloud of dust and gas. Particles at the centre gradually gathered together to make the sun. Those further out formed into the planets. The asteroids may have been prevented from joining together to make a tenth planet by the giant planet, Jupiter. All that is left now of the original cloud are the dust and rocks called meteoroids, and the comets, though nobody really knows how these were formed.

Other moons

Most of the planets have moons circling them. Jupiter's four largest moons were recently visited by two Voyager spacecraft. One of the most interesting moons is called Io. It is bright orange, about the same size as our moon, but with active volcanoes. Voyager found eight very active volcanoes, which were throwing material up to 125 miles above the surface.

Shooting stars

Meteoroids are particles of dust and rock in space. The earth collides with many meteoroids on its journey round the sun. Meteoroids about the size of a small pebble burn up in our atmosphere, leaving fiery trails in the sky called shooting stars. A few are large enough to reach the ground and occasionally they make craters.

Halley's comet

Regular visitor
Comets are strange icy bodies from the edges of the solar system. We can only see them when they travel near the sun and form a huge glowing tail. The tail is thin but very spectacular. The earth passed through the tail of Halley's Comet in 1910 with no ill-effects. Halley's Comet passes close to the sun every 76 years and is next expected in 1986. It was recorded as far back as 1066 on the famous Bayeux Tapestry.

The sun holds its family together by its force of gravity. Most of the planets move round the sun in almost circular paths, called orbits. The moons also circle their parent planets while they travel round the sun. We think of Pluto's orbit as the edge of the solar system, but many of the comets travel far out into the space between the stars. Their orbits also bring them very close to the sun. All the members of the solar system move very fast. The fastest planet is Mercury which races round the sun at 30 m./sec, while the earth moves at 18 m./sec. Compare this with Concorde which flies at just over 1/3 m./sec. The sun, planets and moons also spin as they travel. The earth turns once every day, while Saturn spins in less then ten hours.

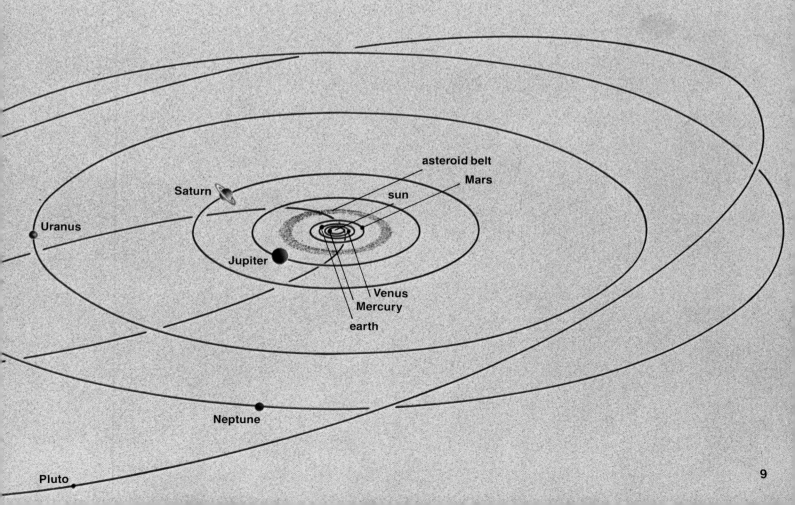

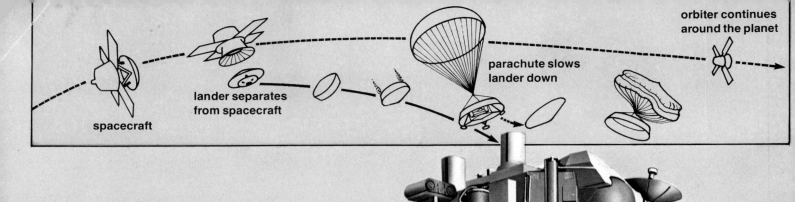

spacecraft

lander separates from spacecraft

parachute slows lander down

orbiter continues around the planet

landing

Exploring the red planet

Mars is often called the 'red planet' because it looks a reddish colour from earth. When the two Viking spacecraft landed on Mars in 1976 their pictures showed that its surface really is red. The red dust is blown up by light winds, and makes the sky look pink. Dust storms can rage over the whole planet. The most exciting task of the Viking landers was to search for life on Mars. They scooped up soil and examined it for signs of simple life. The results puzzled the scientists. They did not find the chemicals that are the basis of life on earth, but this did not mean that there is no life at all on Mars.

Worlds of Rock and Ice

Stars like the sun give out energy and light, but the planets have no light of their own. They only shine by reflecting the light from the sun. The nine planets of our solar system can be divided into two main groups. The four planets nearest the sun are solid balls of rock, while the next four planets are made mainly of liquid and gas. These are known as the 'gas giants'. Pluto, the last planet, is the odd one out. It seems to be a solid ball which may be rocky or even solid ice, and it might once have been a moon of Neptune. Pluto's orbit sometimes brings it nearer the sun than Neptune, but there is no danger of the two planets colliding. Calculations show that they will not come near each other for the next few thousand years.

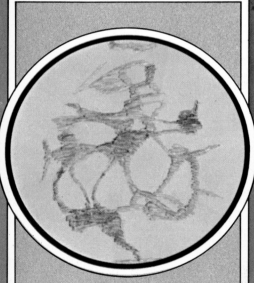

Martian waterways

About 100 years ago an astronomer, Schiaparelli, thought he saw lines on Mars. He called them 'canali', or channels, and thought they were natural features. Others suggested they might be artificial. Lowell thought they were canals built by Martians to irrigate their drying planet. But recent close-up photographs of Mars have proven that no such canals exist.

War of the worlds

H. G. Wells wrote a story about Martians who invaded earth, but were overcome by our earthly germs. Germs from outer space still concern scientists today. The first men on the moon were kept in isolation on their return to earth to ensure that they were not contaminated by 'moon bugs'.

Pioneer astronomers
Tycho Brahe was a 16th-century astronomer who thought that the sun and planets moved round the earth. But his accurate measurements of the planets' orbits helped his successor, Kepler, to work out how the planets moved round the sun.

What is it like on other planets?
The smallest of the planets is either Mercury or Pluto, but Pluto is so far away that we cannot be sure of its size. Mercury is like the moon in some ways; it has no atmosphere and its surface is covered with craters. It is very hot on the side facing the sun and very cold on the other side. Mars is next in size. It has a thin atmosphere, with clouds and fog sometimes visible. Mars also has white polar caps like earth's ice caps. The markings on its surface change with the seasons, so some people thought this must be a sign of plant growth.

Venus and earth have been called sister planets because they are almost the same size, but they are really quite different. Venus has a thick atmosphere of carbon dioxide while ours is mostly nitrogen and oxygen. The water in our seas and atmosphere allows life to flourish. No other planet has seas of water, nor, so far, any sign of life.

Swirling clouds
Venus is a very difficult planet to explore. Its surface is always hidden by thick acid clouds. The pressure at the surface is 92 times that on earth and the temperature is almost high enough to make the rocks glow red.

Early Russian probes to Venus were crushed and baked by the pressure and heat, and probably damaged by the acid. However, in 1975, Venera 9 sent back the first pictures from the rocky surface.

The Gas Giants

Jupiter, Saturn, Uranus and Neptune are often called the 'gas giants', but scientists think they may be mainly liquid planets with thick atmospheres. Both Jupiter and Saturn can be seen with the naked eye. Uranus and Neptune were only discovered in the last 200 years. Uranus was discovered in 1781 by accident when an amateur astronomer, Herschel, was counting stars with his home-made telescope. It was soon noticed that Uranus did not orbit the sun in an expected path and astronomers suggested that another planet was pulling it off course. When mathematicians calculated where this new planet should be, Neptune was easily found. Then it was found that Neptune too did not move as expected, but the culprit, Pluto, was not so easy to find. It was not discovered until 1930. Some people think there may be even more planets beyond Pluto that we have not yet found.

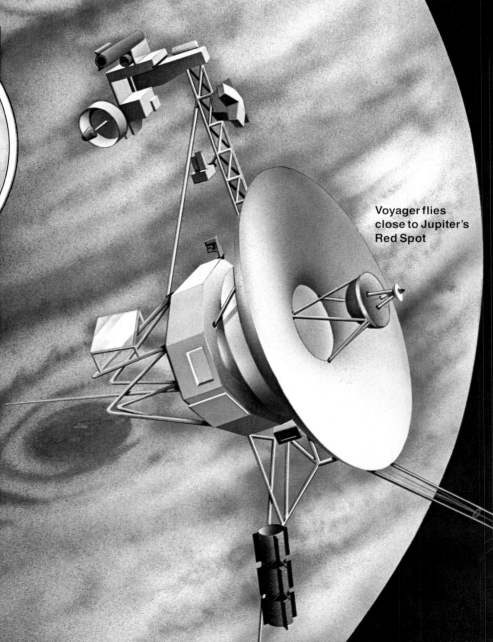

Storms in space

The coloured bands of cloud round Jupiter can easily be seen through telescopes on earth. Spacecraft have sent back clear pictures of the fine patterns in Jupiter's clouds. The Great Red Spot is a higher cooler area of rotating cloud, twice the size of the earth. It is probably a giant storm cloud, like the hurricane in the picture. But it has been raging for centuries. The tops of Jupiter's clouds are very cold. Lower down it is warmer and the atmosphere may contain the ingredients needed for life. The latest Voyager probes sent back pictures showing huge flashes of lightning in Jupiter's atmosphere.

Voyager flies close to Jupiter's Red Spot

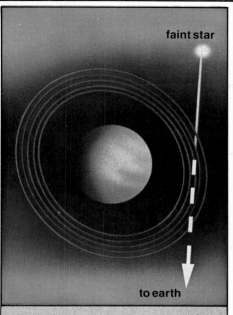

faint star

to earth

Rings around the planets

In 1977, astronomers on earth were watching Uranus pass in front of a faint star. To their amazement the star disappeared and reappeared several times before it reached the planet. The only explanation was that Uranus has a very thin ring system like Saturn has, but it is too faint to be seen from earth. A faint ring system was also discovered round Jupiter by the Voyager spacecraft.

Giants of the solar system

These four planets really are giants. Even the smallest, Neptune, has a diameter about four times that of the earth. Jupiter contains more than twice the material of all the other planets put together. In fact, if Jupiter had been only slightly bigger it would have been a star – it is made of the same gases as the sun. Not only are the 'gas giants' enormous, but the distances between them are also huge. Light from the sun takes about 3 minutes to reach Mercury, 8 minutes to reach earth, but nearly 5 hours to reach Neptune.

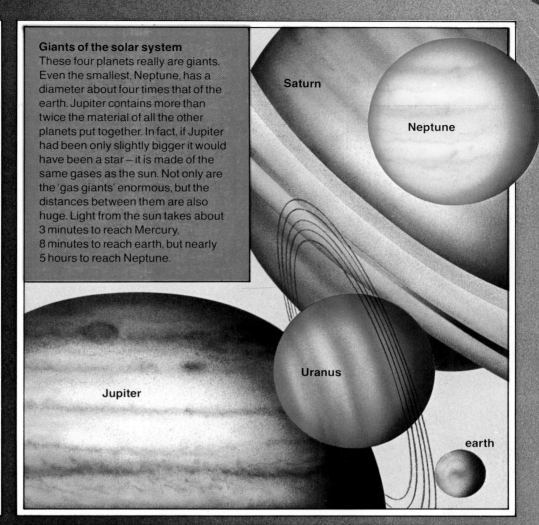

Saturn

Neptune

Uranus

Jupiter

earth

Saturn's rings

Saturn is like Jupiter in many ways, but its ring system is really spectacular. As Saturn moves round the sun, we see the rings at different angles. When they are tilted towards us we can see two bright rings and an inner darker ring. The Pioneer spacecraft that recently visited Saturn found a fourth ring, but it is too dim to be seen from earth. When the rings are edge on to us they can hardly be seen at all because they are so thin. The rings are probably made of small icy chunks circling Saturn. Sometimes stars can be seen shining dimly through them. Saturn is the least dense of the planets – it would float on water if such an experiment were possible.

First Step – the Moon

The earth has only one natural satellite, the moon. It is only about a quarter of the earth's diameter, and is too small to hold an atmosphere. The temperatures on the moon are extreme, ranging from hotter than the Sahara Desert by day to colder than the Antarctic at night.

As our nearest neighbour in space, the moon was the first target for space exploration. In 1959, the first man-made object, Luna 2, crashed onto the moon, and later that year Luna 3 gave us our first glimpse of the farside of the moon. Then, in 1966, Luna 9 became the first probe to land and operate on the moon. These were all Russian spacecraft, but the first man to set foot on the moon in July 1969 was an American, Neil Armstrong.

There have been six successful manned journeys to the moon. The first two astronauts, Armstrong and Aldrin, only stayed a few hours. Later astronauts explored the moon's surface, collecting moon rock and setting up experiments. In one, they listened for moonquakes (earthquakes on the moon), but found the moon very quiet. The last three Apollo missions took lunar rovers with them to the moon. These vehicles carried the astronauts and their equipment over a wide area, in search of different moon rocks. The astronauts wore very bulky space suits to protect them on the moon, so they had to use tongs to pick up the rocks. In the low gravity on the moon, they found it easier to do a kind of kangaroo hop instead of walking. They got into their lunar rovers by jumping upwards and sideways and floating down gently into the seats.

The strange power of the moon
There are many legends and superstitions associated with the moon. One superstition concerns werewolves. These were creatures that looked like humans, but changed into wolves at full moon and attacked people. The full moon was also thought to send some people mad. In fact, the word 'lunatic' comes from the latin word meaning moon.

farside

The moon's farside
The moon moves round the earth once every 27⅓ days, and it spins once on its axis in the same time. So the same side of the moon always faces the earth. This means that we can only study about half the moon from earth. In 1959 Luna 3 sent back the first pictures of the farside. As the moon circles the earth, we see different amounts of the sunlit side, so the moon appears to change in shape. At new moon, the moon is between the sun and the earth and none of the sunlit side is visible. At full moon the earth is between the sun and moon and all the sunlit part can be seen.

Moon and tides

The moon is held in orbit round the earth by the earth's gravity, but the moon's gravity also has an effect on the earth. The moon pulls the surface of the earth towards it, and as the earth is not completely rigid, the surface rises slightly.

The sea tides are also caused by the moon. The differences in water level between high and low tide can be several metres.

Landing problems

The Lunar Module was the part of the spacecraft that landed astronauts on the moon. It was lowered gently onto the moon's surface by landing rockets. It could not use parachutes to slow it down because the moon has no atmosphere. On their return to earth, the astronauts' Command Module entered the atmosphere at very high speed. The atmosphere slowed it, and heated it so that it glowed. It then used parachutes to descend slowly to the sea. Mars has a thin atmosphere, so the Viking spacecraft used parachutes and rockets for a safe landing. The probes to Venus had to travel quickly through its acid clouds. They used their main parachutes when they reached the clear air beneath the clouds.

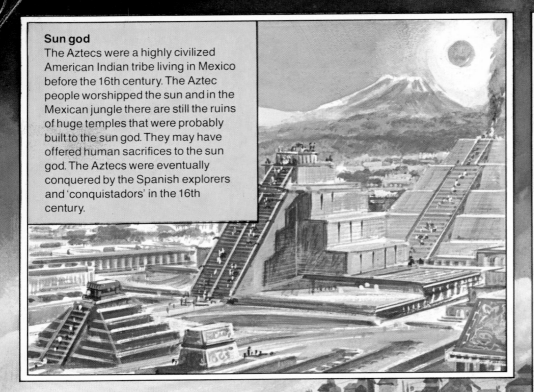

Sun god

The Aztecs were a highly civilized American Indian tribe living in Mexico before the 16th century. The Aztec people worshipped the sun and in the Mexican jungle there are still the ruins of huge temples that were probably built to the sun god. They may have offered human sacrifices to the sun god. The Aztecs were eventually conquered by the Spanish explorers and 'conquistadors' in the 16th century.

The disappearing sun

Occasionally the moon passes directly between the earth and the sun, causing an eclipse. For a few minutes, part of the earth is in the moon's shadow, and the sun is hidden. In ancient times eclipses were greatly feared. The Chinese thought a dragon swallowed the sun, and they tried to scare it away by making loud noises. There is a story that tells how two Chinese astronomers failed to predict an eclipse and were beheaded.

The Life-giver

The sun is just an ordinary star among many millions in our galaxy, but to men on earth it is the source of energy and life. No wonder it was worshipped by many ancient civilizations. It is a huge, hot ball of glowing hydrogen and helium gas, over 100 times the diameter of the earth. This is more than $3\frac{1}{2}$ times the distance between the earth and the moon. The sun contains 750 times as much material as the rest of the solar system put together. It constantly emits energy in the form of heat and light, and it also gives out a stream of particles called the solar wind. The Mariner 10 spacecraft used the solar wind to help it 'sail' on its journey when its fuel was running out.

WARNING – NEVER LOOK AT THE SUN, ESPECIALLY WITH A TELESCOPE OR BINOCULARS. THE LIGHT IS BRIGHT ENOUGH TO BLIND YOU.

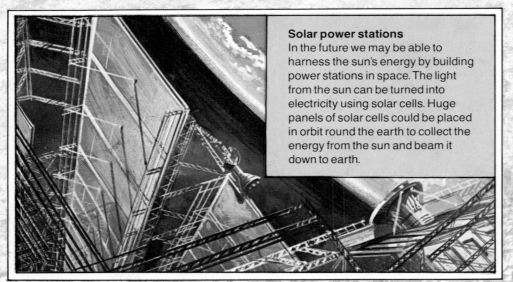

Solar power stations

In the future we may be able to harness the sun's energy by building power stations in space. The light from the sun can be turned into electricity using solar cells. Huge panels of solar cells could be placed in orbit round the earth to collect the energy from the sun and beam it down to earth.

Strange effects

The surface of the sun is constantly churning over. Often, more violent disturbances occur, such as sunspots, prominences and flares. A sunspot is a cooler area that looks dark compared with the rest of the sun. Prominences are eruptions of huge, cool curtains of gas often reaching millions of kilometres above the surface. Solar flares occur near sunspots. They throw out radiation and particles from the sun in short, violent bursts. Flares can affect the earth by interfering with radio communications and causing aurora. Aurora are called the Northern (or Southern) Lights and are displays of moving coloured lights in the sky, near the polar regions. The numbers of sunspots vary from a maximum to a minimum and back, over about eleven years. However, between 1645 and 1715 very few sunspots were recorded. This was the time of the Little Ice Age when the earth had very cold weather – even the River Thames froze over.

prominence

sunspot

aurora

The sun supplies almost all the energy we use. Without sunlight, plants could not grow to provide men and animals with food and oxygen. The coal and oil we use to produce heat and electricity, and to power our vehicles, were once living plants and sea animals, kept alive by the sun. Although we cannot see the centre of the sun where all this energy is created, scientists think it is produced by nuclear reactions. Every second, the sun loses 4 million tons of gas which is turned into energy.

Crab Nebula

Orion Nebula

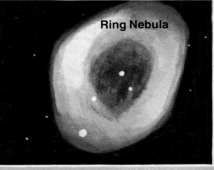

Ring Nebula

Among the stars are great clouds of dust and gas called nebulae. The Crab Nebula is the remains of a star that exploded. Its massive supernova explosion was seen by Chinese astronomers in 1054. The star left at the centre gives out regular pulses of energy and is called a pulsar. The Orion Nebula can be seen with the naked eye. It is the middle 'star' in 'Orion's sword' in the constellation Orion. The Ring Nebula is a shell of glowing gas that was thrown out from its central star.

The Stars

When we look up at the night sky we can only see a few thousand stars, but through the giant modern telescopes many millions of stars can be seen. With a telescope some of these points of light in the sky become fuzzy patches. These are either clouds of dust and gas called nebulae or they are distant galaxies. Stars come in many different sizes. There are giants and supergiants, many times larger than our sun, dwarf stars, about the size of the earth, and tiny neutron stars only a few kilometres across. Many stars have companions, or belong to larger groups. Some star clusters may contain hundreds of thousands of stars. Stars do not all shine steadily like the sun. Some vary regularly in brightness while others occasionally flare up to several times their original brightness.

Future in the stars
Stars were once thought to be gods and many people believed that the stars and planets could influence their lives. During the Middle Ages the Arabs made accurate observations of the planets to try and predict future events. Trying to foretell the future by the positions of the planets is called astrology. But astrology cannot be called a serious science like astronomy.

Sailor's star
At night sailors at sea can use the stars to navigate, or find their way. The Pole Star is almost exactly over the North Pole, so it does not appear to move around the sky as the earth spins, like the other stars. So the Pole Star is a pointer to the north and its position in the sky can tell sailors how far north their ship is.

Story of a star

Stars are born in large spinning clouds of dust and gas. As the cloud collapses, it becomes hotter until nuclear reactions start at the centre. It is then that the star starts shining and will probably shine for billions of years. Our sun is 4½ billion years old and we expect it to shine for another 5 billion years. Eventually all the hydrogen gas in the centre of the star will be used up. It may then expand to become a Red Giant star. Then it will lose its outer layers into space, while the core that is left will shrink to a White Dwarf star, the size of the earth. This will gradually cool and die.

Stars much larger than the sun have shorter and possibly more violent lives. Some end their lives with a huge explosion called a supernova, but these are very rare. Other enormous stars might collapse at the end of their lives to become Black Holes. The material of a Black Hole is packed so tightly that its gravity is enormous and prevents anything, even light, escaping. As nothing can leave a Black Hole we have no direct way of detecting one, but astronomers believe they exist.

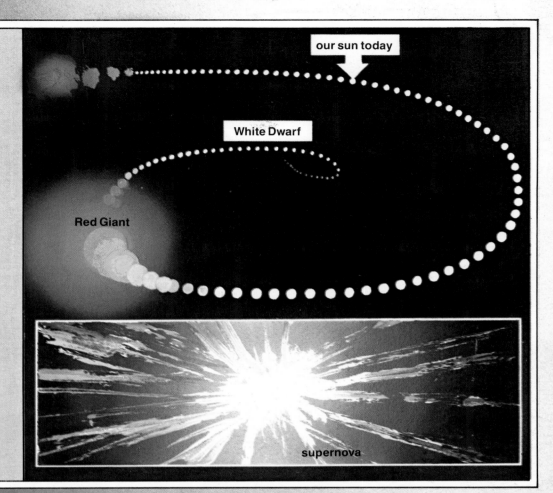

our sun today

White Dwarf

Red Giant

supernova

In about 5 billion years our sun will have burnt up all its hydrogen. It will then probably swell up into a Red Giant star. The centre will collapse, but the outer layers will expand and become cooler and redder. It may even get big enough to swallow up all the planets out as far as Mars. Long before this happens the earth will be too hot to support life. Perhaps our descendants will leave earth in spaceships to find a home on some other planet circling a distant star.

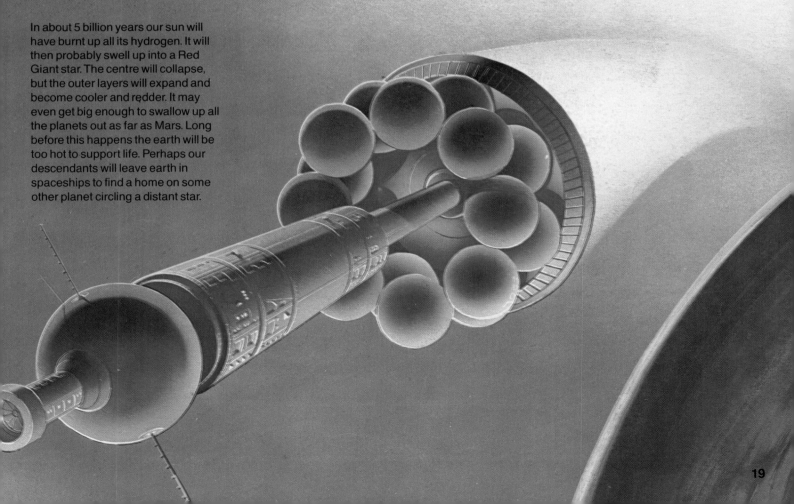

Is Anyone Out There?

One question that fascinates us all is whether there is life anywhere else in the universe. The earth is the only home for life as we know it that we have found in our solar system. However there are probably many planets circling other stars, though these would be too small for us to see, even round the star nearest to us. Out of the thousands of millions of stars in our galaxy and the countless more in further galaxies, it would be surprising if there were not many stars with planets. It is quite possible that there are planets similar to earth where life like ours could develop. Also, there is no reason why life elsewhere should be the same as life on earth. It might be based on different chemicals or it could develop differently in different conditions, just as we have developed to suit the earth's environment.

Studying the stars

Sir William Herschel built his large telescopes to study the stars beyond the solar system. He worked out the shape of our galaxy, the Milky Way, by counting the stars. He also suggested that some of the nebulae among the stars might be galaxies beyond the Milky Way.

Milky Way

Messages from space

If there is intelligent life elsewhere in the universe, perhaps we could communicate with it using a large radio telescope, like this one at Arecibo. The trouble is we do not know where to send messages in outer space. We do not know which stars have planets, or which planet, if any, has intelligent life. We might not even recognize a message if we received one.

Big Bang

Galaxies are groups of thousands of millions of stars. The galaxies themselves are also often grouped into families. Our galaxy is a spiral galaxy, but there are many different shapes. There are different types of spiral galaxies, elliptical (oval) ones and some with no real shape at all. Our largest telescopes can see a thousand million galaxies outside our own and there are probably many more beyond. All the galaxies seem to be moving away from each other at very high speeds. Many astronomers think that this means the universe began with a huge explosion, or Big Bang, which sent the galaxies speeding out in all directions.

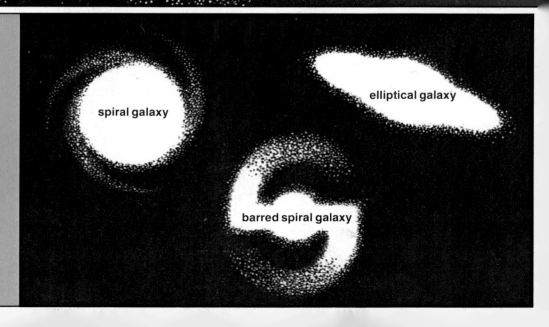

spiral galaxy

elliptical galaxy

barred spiral galaxy

Our galaxy

When you look at the sky at night all the stars you can see are in our galaxy. On a very clear night you can see a faint band of light across the sky. This is the Milky Way, and is the light from many faint stars between us and the centre of our galaxy. The sun is near the edge of the galaxy which is shaped like a flat spiral with a bulge in the middle. We see it edge on so it looks like a flat band of light to us.

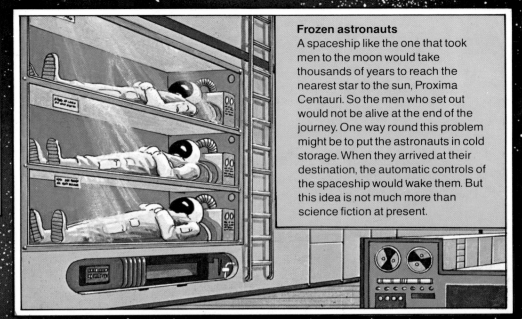

Frozen astronauts

A spaceship like the one that took men to the moon would take thousands of years to reach the nearest star to the sun, Proxima Centauri. So the men who set out would not be alive at the end of the journey. One way round this problem might be to put the astronauts in cold storage. When they arrived at their destination, the automatic controls of the spaceship would wake them. But this idea is not much more than science fiction at present.

Visitors from outer space

Unidentified Flying Objects or UFOs are just strange objects in the sky that cannot be explained. There are many reports of people seeing UFOs, but most of these turn out to be unusual clouds or aircraft. However, a few remain unexplained. Some people believe these are alien spacecraft visiting earth. Some even claim to have talked with beings from outer space.

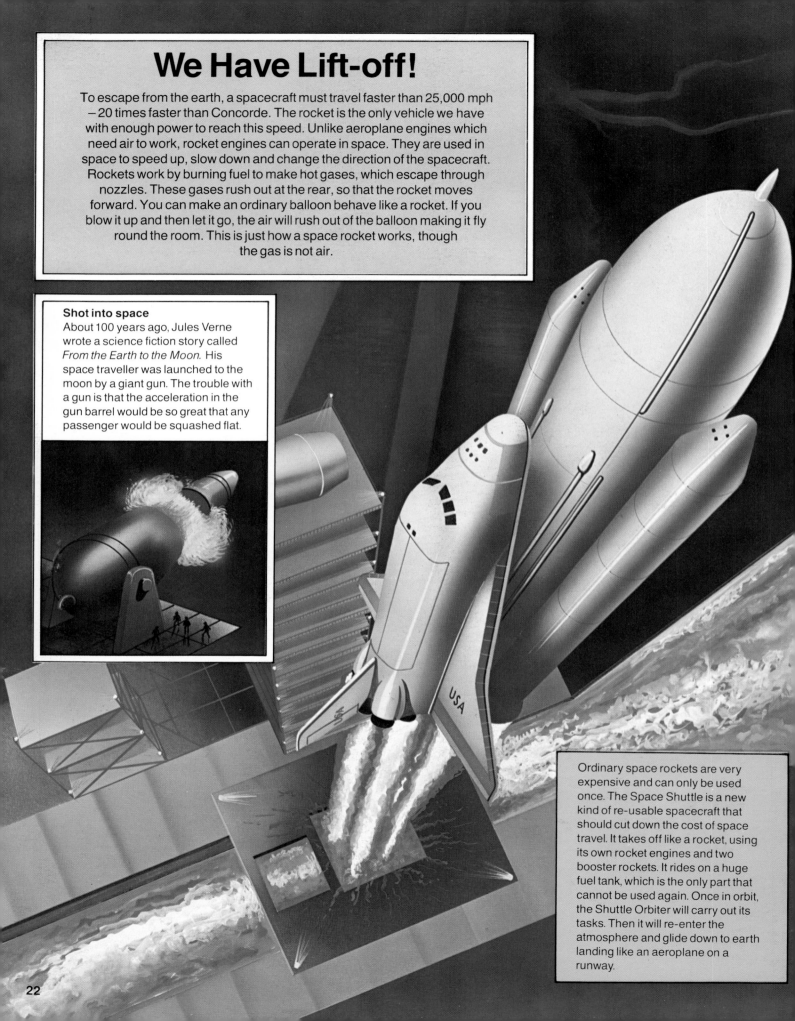

We Have Lift-off!

To escape from the earth, a spacecraft must travel faster than 25,000 mph – 20 times faster than Concorde. The rocket is the only vehicle we have with enough power to reach this speed. Unlike aeroplane engines which need air to work, rocket engines can operate in space. They are used in space to speed up, slow down and change the direction of the spacecraft. Rockets work by burning fuel to make hot gases, which escape through nozzles. These gases rush out at the rear, so that the rocket moves forward. You can make an ordinary balloon behave like a rocket. If you blow it up and then let it go, the air will rush out of the balloon making it fly round the room. This is just how a space rocket works, though the gas is not air.

Shot into space

About 100 years ago, Jules Verne wrote a science fiction story called *From the Earth to the Moon.* His space traveller was launched to the moon by a giant gun. The trouble with a gun is that the acceleration in the gun barrel would be so great that any passenger would be squashed flat.

Ordinary space rockets are very expensive and can only be used once. The Space Shuttle is a new kind of re-usable spacecraft that should cut down the cost of space travel. It takes off like a rocket, using its own rocket engines and two booster rockets. It rides on a huge fuel tank, which is the only part that cannot be used again. Once in orbit, the Shuttle Orbiter will carry out its tasks. Then it will re-enter the atmosphere and glide down to earth landing like an aeroplane on a runway.

Space race

The first rockets were used over 700 years ago by Chinese warriors and were just like the rockets we see at firework displays. However, the first real space rocket was the German V2, used to bombard England during World War II. After this, rockets became bigger and more powerful. Then in 1957, the first satellite, Russia's Sputnik 1, was launched into space. The first man in space was Yuri Gagarin. He flew in 1961 and his launch vehicle was a Vostok rocket. Later that year President Kennedy announced that America would put a man on the moon before 1970. The space race had begun. The first American astronauts were launched by the Mercury-Atlas rocket. The rocket that is still used to launch the Russian Soyuz spacecraft looks like a larger version of the Vostok rocket. Saturn IB is smaller than the giant Saturn V. It was used by both the Apollo and Skylab astronauts.

Saturn 1B

Soyuz

Mercury/Atlas

V2

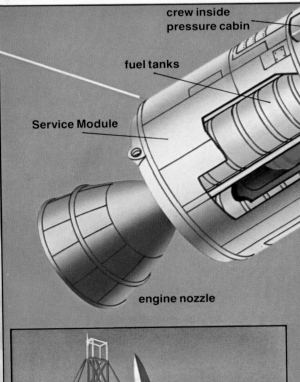

crew inside pressure cabin

fuel tanks

Service Module

Command Module

manoeuvring jets

engine nozzle

The most powerful rocket

The giant Saturn V rocket was built to launch the American astronauts to the moon. At 360 feet tall, it is the biggest rocket ever built. Five engines lifted it off the ground, and each burnt about 950 gallons of fuel every second. This is enough to take an ordinary family car once round the earth's equator.

The Apollo spacecraft that brought men back from the moon was in two parts. The Service Module contained the fuel, engines and supplies. The tiny cone-shaped Command Module carried the men and the spacecraft controls. It held the air for the men to breathe, and its double walls protected them from the dust particles and the cold of space. Its heat shield protected them from the fierce heat when they re-entered the atmosphere.

About half of America's early attempts to launch satellites before 1961 failed. Many ended in spectacular explosions. Later rockets were much safer and all the Saturn rockets that sent men to the moon were successful.

23

Space Travellers

Both Russian cosmonauts and American astronauts have lived for several months in space stations orbiting the earth. But it is not easy to keep people alive and well in space. Our bodies are suited to life on the surface of the earth, held down by the force of gravity. Our atmosphere presses down on us, providing us with air to breathe and protecting us from dangerous radiation from space. When astronauts fly out into space their spacecraft and space suits must hold air for breathing at the right pressure. All their food and water must be brought from earth. Away from the pull of the earth's gravity everything is weightless and doctors feared that this might harm the astronauts. In fact the Skylab astronauts grew slightly taller in space, but they soon returned to normal back on earth and suffered no lasting ill-effects.

Skylab was the first and biggest space station to circle the earth. During its launch in 1973 it was badly damaged, losing a heat shield, so Skylab's first crew became repairmen. Their first task was to put up a specially made sunshade before they could live in the overheated space station. The second was to free a trapped solar panel. Solar panels produce electricity from sunlight, but one had been torn away and another was trapped and useless. Without power from the panels, Skylab's crew could not operate their cameras or much of the equipment needed to carry out their experiments. Luckily, the astronauts managed to free the trapped solar panel, so the Skylab project was saved from failure.

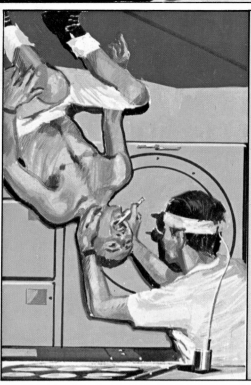

Which way is up?

The most dramatic difference between life on earth and in a space station is weightlessness. In space everything floats and there is no 'up' or 'down'. Skylab astronauts wore special shoes that clipped into grids on the floors and walls so that they could stay in one place to work or eat. They had special sticky foods that stuck to their spoons. They did not need chairs to sit down for meals, and their beds were just sleeping bags fixed to the wall. They seemed to sleep standing up. They took a shower inside a closed bag. Soap and water were carefully rationed because it all had to be brought from earth. Afterwards, the floating drops of water were sucked up with a vacuum hose to stop them floating round the space station. The Skylab astronauts found that regular exercise lessened the effects of weightlessness on their bodies.

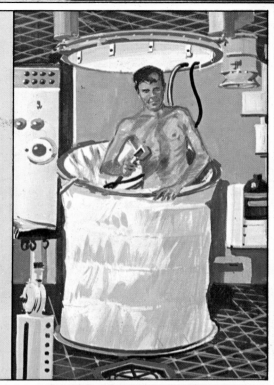

Danger! – Skylab returns

When Skylab was in orbit its speed stopped it from falling straight back to earth. But the force of gravity gradually pulled it into a nearer orbit, so that eventually Skylab plunged into the atmosphere at great speed. It broke up into pieces that raced through the air. Many of them burnt up, but some of the larger pieces fell on earth.

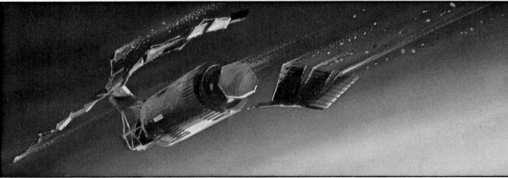

Space link-up

In 1975 Russia and America co-operated in the Apollo-Soyuz spaceflight. An American Apollo spacecraft met and docked with a Russian Soyuz spacecraft in orbit round the earth. The Russians and Americans had worked together closely for over two years to develop a mechanism to fit both spacecraft so that they could link up in space. The astronauts and cosmonauts trained in each other's countries and learned each other's languages.

Robot Explorers

The men who went to the moon and the astronauts who lived in space stations for months made sensational news, but most of the work of exploring space is done by unmanned robot spacecraft. These have visited all but the three outer planets, and have landed on the moon, Venus and Mars. Mariner 9 circled Mars mapping the whole surface of the planet. Now two Pioneer and two Voyager spacecraft have crossed the asteroid belt to visit the giant outer planets, Jupiter and Saturn. Eventually Voyager 2 may send back information from Uranus more than eight years after leaving earth. At present we could not send men on space journeys this long because of the dangers of radiation and possible spacecraft failure. During the last 20 years robot explorers have greatly increased our knowledge of the solar system.

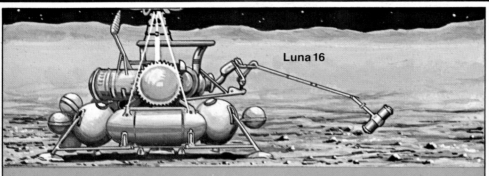

Luna 16

Collecting moon rock
Luna 16 was a Russian robot spacecraft that brought soil samples back from the moon. It landed on the moon in 1970 and collected a few ounces of lunar soil. This was a much smaller amount than that brought back by the Apollo moon astronauts. On the other hand, Luna 16 was probably cheaper to send into space.

Television from space
Satellites circling the earth now form part of our everyday lives. Communications satellites connect us to other continents by telephone links. They can beam live television programmes right round the world. Weather satellites, like this Russian one called Meteor, watch our atmosphere. The information they collect helps the weather forecasters.

Robots under the sea
Robot submarines are used where it is difficult for men to work. Like space probes they use television cameras for eyes and are controlled by engineers on earth. But submarines work in deep water at very high pressures while there is no pressure in the emptiness of space.

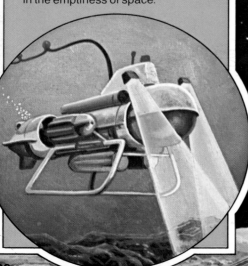

Lunokhod was the first 'mooncar'. It landed in 1970 and crawled over the moon's surface for nearly a year. It was controlled by a team of scientists in Russia, who watched the pictures from its television cameras and sent radio commands to steer it. Lunokhod's instruments measured the chemicals that made up moon rocks.

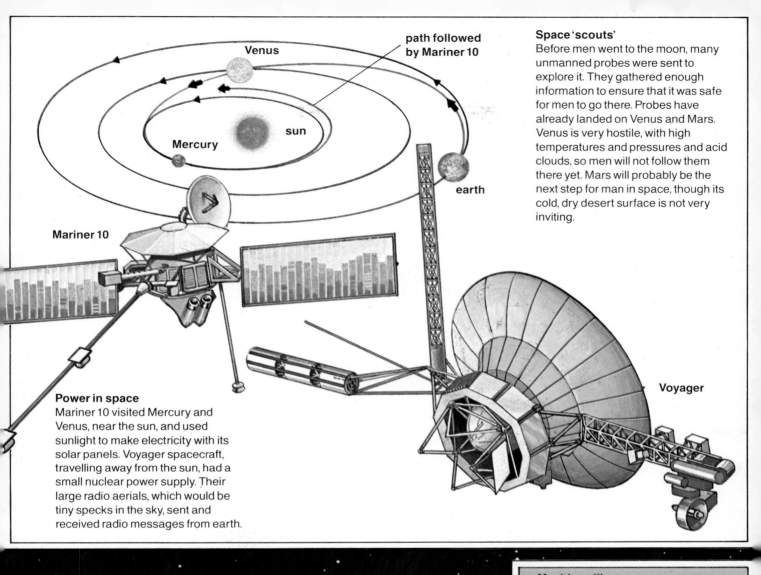

Venus

path followed by Mariner 10

sun

Mercury

earth

Mariner 10

Space 'scouts'
Before men went to the moon, many unmanned probes were sent to explore it. They gathered enough information to ensure that it was safe for men to go there. Probes have already landed on Venus and Mars. Venus is very hostile, with high temperatures and pressures and acid clouds, so men will not follow them there yet. Mars will probably be the next step for man in space, though its cold, dry desert surface is not very inviting.

Voyager

Power in space
Mariner 10 visited Mercury and Venus, near the sun, and used sunlight to make electricity with its solar panels. Voyager spacecraft, travelling away from the sun, had a small nuclear power supply. Their large radio aerials, which would be tiny specks in the sky, sent and received radio messages from earth.

Machines like men
Robots in fiction, like C3PIO from the film *Star Wars,* are often made to look like humans, but this is not practical in real life. Lunokhod used cameras for eyes and its wheels were simpler than legs. Luna 16 had a drill on the end of a mechanical arm to pick up moon rock.

Lunokhod

Space Stations

There have been great steps forward in space exploration in a very short time. It took only twelve years from the launch of Sputnik 1, the first object to escape from the earth, to the first manned landing on the moon. Astronauts have now lived and worked in space stations for months. But we have not really travelled far from home in terms of the vast distances in space. In the future astronauts will travel to other planets in our solar system in spite of the enormous distances. With our present spacecraft it takes months to reach Mars, one of the nearest planets, and years to reach Jupiter and the outer planets. At this speed it would take thousands of years to reach the nearest star. So our immediate future in space will probably be in space stations near the earth or colonies on the moon or planets.

Indoor space gardens
A space station of the future might be shaped like a huge spinning wheel, where people could spend their whole lives. Living plants could be an important part of a space community. People take oxygen gas out of the air when they breathe, giving out carbon dioxide gas. Plants use up the carbon dioxide and replace the oxygen. So, in a closed space station growing plants could be used to replace the oxygen taken out of the air by people. The plants could also be used for food. So a space station could produce its own food and power. But materials for repairs or building would have to be brought from earth or other planets.

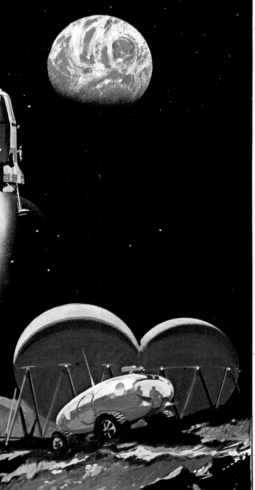

In the distant future we may build space stations in earth orbit as permanent homes. Up to now everything sent into space has been built on earth. But the parts for a large space station would probably be made on earth and put together in space over a period of years. The problem of weightlessness for the people living in a space station could be overcome by making the space station spin slowly. This would produce a force similar to gravity on earth. A large space station could be almost self-sufficient, for its power would be produced from the sunlight using solar panels.

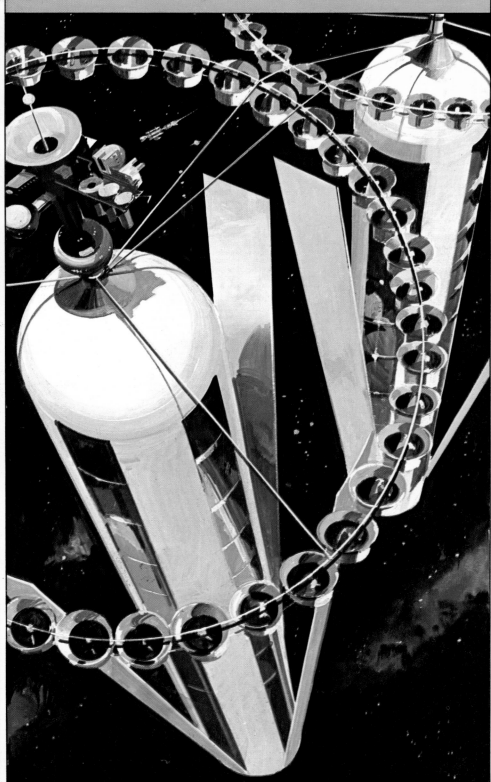

As we use up the minerals in the earth's rocks, it may become economical to collect raw materials from the moon or planets. Then we would have to build colonies to house people and their equipment. Colonies could be built on the moon or the rocky planets like Mars, or on the moons of the larger planets. One of the first buildings on the moon will probably be an observatory. A telescope on the moon will be able to collect more information than one on earth where our atmosphere gets in the way. Astronomers there might even be able to use a telescope during daylight. On earth the sunlight is scattered by the atmosphere and swamps the starlight. On the moon there is no real atmosphere, but dust may prevent daylight observation.

Some useful words

Asteroids Very small planets that circle the sun mainly in a belt between Jupiter and Mars.

Atmosphere A layer of gases round a planet. The atmosphere of each planet has a different mixture of gases.

Comets Icy bodies, sometimes called 'dirty snowballs', that circle the sun. They form long glowing tails when they come near the sun.

Constellation A group of stars that form a pattern in the sky.

Crater A nearly circular dip in the ground. Some of the craters on the moon were made by falling meteoroids.

Galaxy A group or family of stars containing hundreds of millions of stars.

Gravity A force that pulls one body towards another. Gravity holds us on to the surface of the earth, and keeps the earth in orbit round the sun.

Meteoroids Small rocks or dust in space.

Milky Way A band of light across the sky given out by millions of stars between us and the centre of our galaxy.

Moon A smaller body circling a planet.

Nebula A cloud of dust and gases in space.

Orbit The path of one body round another in space. The moon is in orbit round the earth, which is in orbit round the sun.

Planet A body circling a star. Some of those circling the sun are rocky and others are liquid and gas. Planets have no light of their own, but reflect sunlight.

Satellite An artificial or natural object that circles another body. The earth has one natural satellite, the moon, and many artificial ones.

Solar system The sun and its family of circling objects including planets, moons and comets.

Star A ball of very hot glowing gases which creates energy and gives it out mainly in the form of light.

Sun The nearest star to us.

Telescope An instrument that collects information such as light or radio waves from space.

Universe Everything in space that we know about, including our solar system, stars, galaxies and nebulae.

The Sky at Night

To see the sky at night in all its beauty you must choose a clear dark night. You should also get away from towns into the open where there are no street lights to swamp the faint starlight. The stars make patterns in the sky called constellations. These appear to move, because of the earth's movements in space. They move across the sky during the night as the earth spins, and appear in different parts of the sky at different times of year. The planets move across the star patterns so they are more difficult to find. Some newspapers have monthly star maps which tell you where to look for certain planets. If you look up in the western sky, just after sunset, you can be fairly sure that the bright star that sometimes appears there before any other star, is Venus. Mars can be recognized by its red colour.

Improved sight

A pair of binoculars can show you some more wonders of the night sky. With them you will be able to see the craters on the moon. The four largest moons of Jupiter will appear as little dots near the bright disc of the planet, and the Milky Way will reveal many separate stars. You can also see that the Orion Nebula is not a star but a fuzzy patch of light.

Some useful books

Ardley. *Man and Space.* Macdonald Educational.

Becklake. Exploration and Discovery, *Man and the Moon.* Macmillan Children's Books.

Becklake. Exploration and Discovery, *The Solar System.* Macmillan Children's Books.

Gatland. *Exploring Space.* Macdonald Educational.

Kerrod. *The Universe.* Sampson Low.

Moore. *Man the Astronomer.* Priory Press.

Moore. *The Observer's Book of Astronomy.* Frederick Warne & Co.

Siefarth. Junior Knowledge, *Space Travel.* Lutterworth.

Schmidt. Junior Knowledge, *Astronomy.* Lutterworth.

Places to visit

Major museums holding permanent exhibitions on astronomy and space include:

The Science Museum, London.

Royal Scottish Museum, Edinburgh, Scotland.

Merseyside County Museums, Liverpool.

National Maritime Museum, Greenwich, London.

Planetaria screen shows of the sky at night. Some planetaria are not open all the year round, and most have astronomy and space exhibitions.

The London Planetarium, London, NW1.

Science Museum Planetarium, London, SW7.

Merseyside County Museums Planetarium, Liverpool.

Armagh Planetarium, Armagh, N. Ireland.

Greenwich Planetarium, National Maritime Museum, Greenwich, London, SE10.

Jodrell Bank Planetarium, Jodrell Bank, Macclesfield, Cheshire.

The observatories listed below are open to the public at various times:

Royal Greenwich Observatory, Herstmonceux, Sussex.

Royal Observatory, Edinburgh, Scotland.

Jodrell Bank Radio Astronomy Laboratories, Jodrell Bank, Macclesfield, Cheshire.

Clubs to join

British Astronomical Association, Junior Section, Burlington House, Piccadilly, London SW1V 2JJ.

British Interplanetary Society, 27/29 South Lambeth Road, London SW8 1SZ. Most large towns have amateur astronomical societies for those interested in looking at the night sky. Your local library should be able to help you find them.

Northern sky

Cetus
Aquarius
Pisces
Capricorn
Aries
Eridanus
Pegasus
Delphinus
Pleiades
Taurus
Sagittarius
Cassiopeia
Cygnus
Orion
Rigel
Cepheus
Perseus
Lyra
Lepus
Betelgeuse
Pole star (Polaris)
Draco
Little Bear
Gemini
Ophiuchus
Canis Major
Hercules
Sirius
Corona Borealis
Canis Minor
Scorpio
Serpens
Great Bear
Libra
Boötes
Leo
Virgo
Crater
Corvus
Hydra

Star-gazing

Some of the constellations are only visible from the northern hemisphere, while others can be seen only from the south. Orion is a bright constellation that is seen in the north in winter and in the south in summer. The three stars of Orion's belt surrounded by four bright stars are easily found. Betelgeuse (pronounced beetle juice!) at the top left and Rigel at the bottom right are both Red Giant stars. Hanging from Orion's belt is his sword. You can see that the middle of the three sword stars is not really a star but a fuzzy patch of light. This is the Great Nebula, a cloud of dust and gas where new stars are born. Another cluster of young stars is the Pleiades. These can be found by looking up and right a little way from Orion. On the other side of Orion is Sirius, the Dog Star, the brightest star in the sky. Observers in the north will be able to see the bright W of Cassiopeia all through the year. The best known southern constellation is the Southern Cross. Near it are two bright stars and the one away from the cross is Alpha (Proxima) Centauri, the nearest star to the sun.

Southern sky

Aries
Pisces
Pleiades
Aquarius
Delphinus
Taurus
Cygnus
Phoenix
Eridanus
Grus
Indus
Lyra
Rigel
Tucana
Lepus
Dorado
Sagittarius
Betelgeuse
Ophiuchus
Orion
Columba
Canis Major
Carina
Scorpio
Sirius
Southern cross (Crux)
Puppis
Alpha (Proxima) Centauri
Gemini
Hercules
Canis Minor
Hydra
Libra
Crater
Serpens
Corvus
Corona Borealis
Virgo
Boötes
Leo

A fixed star?

The Pole Star is almost over the North Pole so it seems to stand still. The easiest way to find it is to locate the constellation known as the Plough, or Great Bear. Look along the seven bright stars that form the ladle shape. The last two of these stars point directly to the Pole Star.

Little Bear
Pole Star
Great Bear

Index

Aldrin, Edwin 'Buzz' 14
Alpha (Proxima) Centauri 21, 31
Apollo missions 14, 23, 26
Apollo-Soyuz link-up 25
Arabs 18
Arecibo radio telescope 20
Armstrong, Neil 14
Asteroids 8, 26
Astrology 18
Astronomers, amateur 6
  pioneer 6-7, 11-12
Aurora 17
Aztecs 16

Bayeux Tapestry 9
Betelgeuse 31
Big Bang 20
Black Hole 19
Brahe, Tycho 11

Cassiopeia 31
China 16, 18, 23
Coal 17
Columbus, Christopher 5
Colonies, space 28-9
Comets 7, 9
Communications satellites 26
Conquistadors 16
Crab Nebula 18

Deimos 8
Dog Star 31
Dwarf stars 18, 19

Earth, as centre of universe 5, 11
  flat or round 5
Eclipses 4, 16
Egyptians, Ancient 5

From the Earth to the Moon (Verne) 22

Galaxies 18, 20-21
Galileo Galilei 6
Gagarin, Yuri 23
Germs, from outer space 10
Gravity 9, 14, 19, 24, 25
Great Bear 31
Great (Orion) Nebula 18, 30, 31
Greeks, Ancient 5

Halley's Comet 9
Herschel, Sir William 12, 20

India 5, 6
Io 8

Jupiter 8, 12, 13, 26, 28, 31

Kennedy, President 23
Kepler, Johann 11

Little Ice Age 17
Luna spacecraft 14, 26

Lunar modules 15
Lunar rovers 14
Lunokhod 26, 27

Mariner spacecraft 16, 26, 27
Mars 8, 10, 11, 15, 19, 26, 27, 28, 30
  canals 10
Mercury 9, 11, 13, 27
Mercury-Atlas rocket 23
Meteor satellite 26
Meteoroids 8
Mexico 16
Milky Way 20, 31
Moon 6, 14-15, 26, 27
Moon rock 26
Moons (around planets other than earth) 8

Navigation by stars 18
Nebulae 18, 20, 30, 31
Neptune 10, 12, 13
Northern Lights (aurora) 17
Nova 6
Nuclear reactions 17, 19
Nut, Egyptian sky goddess 5

Oil 17
Orbits, planetary 9
Orion 18, 31
  nebula 18, 30, 31

Pioneer spacecraft 13, 26
Pleiades 31
Plough 31
Pluto 9, 10, 11, 12
Pole Star 18, 31
Proxima Centauri 21, 31
Ptolemy 5
Pulsars 7, 18

Ra, Egyptian sun god 5
Radiation 6
Radio telescopes 6-7, 20
Radio waves 6-7
Red Giant 19, 31
Rigel 31
Ring Nebula 18
Robot spacecraft 26-7
Rockets 22-3

Sacrifice, human 16
Satellites 23, 26
Saturn 8, 12, 13, 26
Saturn rockets 23
Schiaparelli 10
Science fiction 10, 22, 27
Shooting stars 8
Sirius 31
Skylab 23, 24-5
Solar energy 16
Solar flares 17
Solar prominences 17
Solar system 8-9
Southern Cross 31
Southern Lights (aurora) 17
Soyuz spacecraft 23, 25

Space probes 6, *see also under individual names*
Space Shuttle 22
Space stations 24-5, 28-9
Space travel 14-15, 20-29
Sputnik 1 23, 28
Star Wars, film 27
Stars 18-19
Stone Age 4-5
Stonehenge 4-5
Submarines, robot 26
Sun 8, 16-17
Sun gods 4, 5, 16
Sunspots 17
Supernovae 18, 19
Superstitions 4-5, 14, 16

Telescopes 6-7, 20, 28
Thames, river 17
Tides 14

USA 15, 23, 24-5, 26-7
USSR 14, 23, 24, 25, 26
Unidentified Flying Objects (UFOs) 21
Uranus 8, 12, 13

V2 rocket 23
Venera probes 11
Venus 11, 15, 26, 27, 30
Verne, Jules 22
Viking spacecraft 10, 15
Volcanoes 8
Vostok rocket 23
Voyager spacecraft 8, 12, 13, 26, 27

Weather forecasting 26
Weightlessness 24-5, 29
Wells, H.G. 10
Werewolves 14
White Dwarf 19
World War II 23

The space stations that appear on pages 28 and 29 are based on plans drawn up by the National Aeronautics and Space Administration (NASA).